Oxford Reading Tree

Group Activity Sheets

Book 2 for Stages 4 and 5

Thelma Page and Kay Su

Great Clarendon Street, Oxford OX2 6DP

Oxford University Press is a department of the University of Oxford. It furthers the University's objective of excellence in research, scholarship, and education by publishing worldwide in

Oxford New York

Auckland Bangkok Buenos Aires Cape Town Chennai Dar es Salaam Delhi Hong Kong Istanbul Karachi Kolkata Kuala Lumpur Madrid Melbourne Mexico City Mumbai Nairobi São Paulo Shanghai Taipei Tokyo Toronto

First published 1999

10 9 8 7 6 5 4 3 2

ISBN 0 19 918960 9

Illustrations by Jan Brychta, cover illustration by Alex Brychta

Printed in the UK by Athenæum Press Ltd, Gateshead, Tyne & Wear

Contents

Year 1 Term 3

Stage 5

Introduction

The activities in this book have been planned to meet the requirements of the National Literacy Strategy Framework. Within the Literacy Hour, there is time each day for children to work on individual activities while the teacher reads with a group. These copymasters provide focused individual work to reinforce current class and group teaching objectives. Where the activity needs adult help, the page is marked (A). Where it is hoped that the child will be able to work independently, the page is marked (I).

The copymasters build upon the activities and suggestions provided in the Teacher's Guides. They use the child's involvement with the characters and the stories of the *Oxford Reading Tree* to practise and reinforce the skills and knowledge required by the NLS Framework.

The teaching objectives are taken directly from the National Literacy Strategy Framework document. The yearly and termly expectations are matched to *Oxford Reading Tree* stories:

Year 1 Term 2: Stage 4 stories

1 *House For Sale*	4 *The Secret Room*
2 *The New House*	5 *The Play*
3 *Come In!*	6 *The Storm*

Year 1 Term 3: Stage 5 stories

1 *The Magic Key*	4 *Gran*
2 *Pirate Adventure*	5 *Castle Adventure*
3 *The Dragon Tree*	6 *Village in the Snow*

For each book there are three worksheets, aimed at Word level **W**, Sentence level **S** and Text level **T** teaching objectives. There is also a sheet of notes for each book showing the Main learning outcome, explaining what to do and suggesting a further activity for more able children. The level of difficulty is intended for children of average ability at each stage. Less able children may need the support of an adult. Alternatively, the teacher could use the sheets as part of his or her guided reading time with a group needing more help.

Coverage and Record Keeping

Pages 6–10 list the teaching objectives for Year 1 Term 2 and Year 1 Term 3. The bold page numbers show the copymaster appropriate to the objective. The italic page numbers indicate a suggestion for a further activity related to that objective. The remaining columns enable you to keep a record of work covered with a group of six children.

Further copymasters

These have been planned to allow for coverage of teaching objectives not covered by the story-related sheets. They include work requiring reference to more than one book, making comparisons, expressing preferences and using poetry and non-fiction. At Stage 5 they also include more material to practise phonemes and spelling patterns.

Assessment

The assessment pages include word building, using blends and double vowel phonemes, understanding of the term 'phoneme', high frequency word recognition and the ability to write complete sentences. The sheets, together with observation notes by the teacher, will form a record of progress. Where possible, suggestions have been included to enable the children to be involved in recording their own attainment. In addition, any copymaster could be used to assess a child's response to a particular teaching objective.

General notes

- It is vital that the copymasters are selected to reinforce current teaching objectives from shared and guided reading sessions.
- The children should have a clear idea of the purpose of the activity as well as understanding the task.
- The work check face is for children to colour when they have finished and checked their work.
- Although there is some overlap between *Oxford Reading Tree* words and high frequency words from Appendix List 1 of the NLS Framework, the words are listed separately for assessment.
- The copymasters reflect the spiral approach of the NLS Framework in returning to basic teaching objectives to reinforce them before moving on.
- The objectives not covered by the copymasters are those based upon oral work such as read ing with expression or role play.

Involving parents

Although the copymasters are not intended to provide reading homework for the children, teachers will find some sheets, such as the high frequency word lists and the *Oxford Reading Tree* key words, useful to cut up and send home for extra practice.

NLS record of achievement for Year 1 Term 2

Word level work

Phonics, spelling and vocabulary	**Pages**	**Names**					
Phonological awareness, phonics and spelling 1 to secure identification, spelling and reading of initial, final and medial letter sounds in simple words	**48**						
2 to investigate, read and spell words ending in *ff, ll, ss, ck, ng*	**32 49**						
3 to discriminate, read and spell words with initial consonant clusters, e.g. *bl, cr, tr, str* Appendix List 3	*27 31* **28 50**						
to discriminate, read and spell words with final consonant clusters, e.g. *nd, lp, st* Appendix List 3	**51**						
to identify separate phonemes within words containing clusters, in speech and writing	*27 31*						
to blend phonemes in words with clusters for reading							
to segment clusters into phonemes for spelling	*27*						
Word recognition, graphic knowledge and spelling 4 for guided reading, read on sight high frequency words specific to graded books matched to the abilities of reading groups	(TG2) *11 23* **52**						
5 to read on sight other familiar words, e.g. children's names, equipment labels, classroom captions	*15*						
6 to read on sight approximately 30 more high frequency words from Appendix List 1	*19* **20 92–95**						
7 to recognize critical features of words, e.g. length, common spelling patterns and words within words	**24**						
8 to investigate and learn spellings with 's' for plurals	(TG2)						
9 to spell common irregular words from Appendix List 1	**12 92–95**						
Vocabulary extension 10 new words from reading and shared experiences; make collections of words of personal interest or significant words and words linked to particular topics	**16**						
Handwriting 11 to practise handwriting in conjunction with spelling and independent writing, ensuring correct letter orientation, formation and proportion, in a style that makes the letters easy to join later.	**79**						

Sentence level work

Grammar and punctuation							
Grammatical awareness 1 to expect reading to make sense and check if it does not, and to read aloud using expression appropriate to the grammar of the text	*27* **21**						
2 to use awareness of grammar of a sentence to decipher new or unfamiliar words, e.g. to predict text from the grammar, read on, leave a gap and re-read	**13**						
3 to predict words from preceding words in sentences, and investigate the sorts of words that would fit, suggesting appropriate alternatives, i.e. that make sense	*23* **13 25**						
Sentence construction and punctuation 4 to recognize full stops and capital letters when reading and understand how they affect the way a passage is read	**21**						

	Pages	Names					
5 to continue demarcating sentences in writing, ending a sentence with a full stop	*11 15 19 31*						
6 to use the term *sentence* appropriately to identify sentences in text, i.e. those demarcated by capital letters and full stops	**29**						
7 to use a capital letter for the personal pronoun 'I', for names, and for the start of a sentence.	*19 27* **33**						

Text level work

Fiction and poetry							
Reading comprehension 1 to reinforce and apply word level skills through shared and guided reading							
2 to use phonological, contextual, grammatical and graphic knowledge to work out, predict and check the meaning of unfamiliar words and to make sense of what they read							
3 to choose and read familiar books with concentration and attention, discuss preferences and give reasons	*35* **37** (TG2)						
4 to re-tell stories, giving the main points in sequence and notice the difference between spoken and written forms in re-telling, e.g. by comparing oral versions with the written text; to refer to relevant phrases and sentences	*31* **22**						
5 to identify and record some key features of story language from a range of stories, and to practise reading and using them, e.g. in oral re-tellings	*23*						
6 to identify and discuss a range of story themes, and to collect and compare	*35* **38**						
7 to discuss reasons for, and causes of, incidents in stories	**34**						
8 to identify and discuss characters, e.g. from appearance, behaviour, qualities; to speculate about how they might behave; to discuss how they are described in the text; and to compare characters from different stories or plays	*35* **39**						
9 become aware of character and dialogue, e.g. by role-playing parts when reading aloud stories or plays							
10 to identify and compare basic story elements, e.g. beginnings and endings in different stories	*35* **40**						
11 to learn and recite simple poems and rhymes, with actions, and to re-read from the text							
Writing composition 12 through shared and guided writing to apply phonological, graphic knowledge and sight vocabulary to spell words accurately	*11 19 27*						
13 to substitute and extend patterns from reading through language play, e.g. by using the same lines and introducing new words, extending rhyming or alliterative patterns, adding further rhyming words and sentences from text	*35* **41**						
14 to represent outlines of story plots using, e.g. captions, pictures, arrows to record main incidents in order, e.g. make a class book, wall story, own version	**18 26**						
15 to build simple profiles of characters from stories read, describing characteristics, appearances, behaviour, using pictures, single words, captions, words and sentences from text	**14**						
16 to use some of the elements of known stories to structure own writing	*15* **22 30**						

Non-fiction	Pages	Names						
Reading comprehension 17 to use the terms 'fiction' and 'non-fiction', noting some of their differing features, e.g. layout, titles, contents page, use of pictures, labelled diagrams	**42**							
18 to read non-fiction books and understand that the reader doesn't need to go from start to finish but selects according to what is needed								
19 to predict what a given book might be about from a brief look at both the front and the back covers, including blurb, title, illustration; to discuss what it might tell in advance of reading and check to see if it does								
20 to use simple dictionaries, and to understand their alphabetical organization	*36* **43**							
21 to understand the purpose of contents pages and indexes and begin to locate information by page numbers and words by initial letter								
Writing composition 22 to write labels for drawings and diagrams, e.g. growing beans, parts of the body								
23 to produce extended captions, e.g. to explain paintings in wall displays or to describe artefacts								
24 to write simple questions, e.g. as part of an interactive display (How many . . . ? Where is . . . ?)	*36* **44**							
25 to assemble information from own experience, e.g. food, pets; to use simple sentences to describe, based on examples from reading; to write simple non-chronological reports; to organize lists, separate pages, charts.	*36* **45**							

NLS record of achievement for Year 1 Term 3

Word level work

Phonics, spelling and vocabulary	Pages	Names						
Phonological awareness, phonics and spelling 1 the common spelling patterns for each of the long vowel phonemes ee, *ai, ie, oa, oo* (as in 'moon') Appendix List 3:	*57 73 61* **62 74 78 84 85 86**							
to identify phonemes in speech and writing	**74**							
to blend phonemes for reading								
to segment words into phonemes for spelling	*53 57*							
Word recognition, graphic knowledge and spelling 2 to read on sight high frequency words specific to graded books matched to the abilities of reading groups	**89** (TG2)							
3 to read on sight other familiar words								
4 to read on sight approximately 30 more high frequency words from Appendix List 1	**70 92–95**							
5 to recognize words by common spelling patterns	**54**							
6 to investigate and learn spellings of verbs with 'ed' (past tense), 'ing' (present tense endings)	**66**							
7 to spell common irregular words from Appendix List 1	*65*							

	Pages	Names					
Vocabulary extension 8 new words from reading and shared experiences; make collections of words of personal interest or significant words and words linked to particular topics	*69*						
9 the terms 'vowel' and 'consonant'	**58**						
Handwriting 10 to practise handwriting in conjunction with spelling (above) and independent writing, ensuring correct letter orientation, formation and proportion, in a style that makes the letters easy to join later	**79**						

Sentence level work

Grammar and punctuation							
Grammatical awareness 1 to expect reading to make sense and check if it does not	**55**						
2 to use awareness of grammar of a sentence to decipher new or unfamiliar words, e.g. to predict text from the grammar, read on, leave a gap and re-read	*53* **75**						
3 to read familiar texts aloud with pace and expression appropriate to the grammar, e.g. pausing at full stops, raising voice for questions							
4 about word order, e.g. by re-ordering sentences, predicting words from previous text, grouping a range of words that might 'fit', and discussing the reasons why	**63**						
Sentence construction and punctuation 5 other common uses of capitalization, e.g. for personal titles (Mr, Miss) headings, book titles, emphasis	**67**						
6 through reading and writing, to reinforce knowledge of the term *sentence* from previous terms	*61 73* **59 90 91**						
7 to add question marks to questions.	*57* **71**						

Text level work

Comprehension and composition							
Fiction and poetry **Reading comprehension** 1 to reinforce and apply word level skills through shared and guided reading							
2 to use phonological, contextual, grammatical and graphic knowledge to work out, predict and check the meaning of unfamiliar words and to make sense of what they read							
3 to notice the difference between spoken and written forms through re-telling known stories; compare oral versions with the written text							
4 to read with sufficient concentration to complete a text, and to identify preferences and give reasons							
5 to re-tell stories, to give the main points in sequence and to pick out significant incidents	**76**						
6 to prepare and re-tell stories orally, identifying and using some of the more formal features of story language							
7 to use titles, cover pages, pictures and 'blurbs' to predict the content of unfamiliar stories	**68**						

	Pages	Names					
8 to compare and contrast stories with a variety of settings, e.g. space, imaginary lands, animal homes	**80**						
9 to read a variety of poems on similar themes, e.g. families, school, food							
10 to compare and contrast preferences and common themes in stories and poems	**81**						
11 to collect class and individual favourite poems for class anthologies, participate in reading aloud							
Writing composition 12 through shared and guided writing to apply phonological, graphic knowledge and sight vocabulary to spell words accurately	*53 65*						
13 to write about significant incidents from known stories	**56**						
14 to write stories using simple settings, e.g. based on previous reading	*61*						
15 to use poems or parts of poems as models for own writing, e.g. by substituting words or elaborating on the text	**82**						
16 to compose own poetic sentences, using repetitive patterns, carefully selected sentences and imagery	**72**						
Non-fiction **Reading comprehension** 17 to recognize that non-fiction books on similar themes can give different information and present similar information in different ways							
18 to read recounts and begin to recognize generic structure, e.g. ordered sequence of events, use of words like *first, next, after, when*	*69* **60**						
19 to identify simple questions and use text to find the answers. To locate parts of text that give particular information including labelled diagrams and charts, e.g. *parts of a car, what pets eat, clothes that keep us warm*	*73*						
Writing composition 20 to write simple recounts linked to topics of interest/study or to personal experience, using the language of texts read as models for own writing. Make class/group books, e.g. *Our day at school, Our trip to . . .*							
21 to use the language and features of non-fiction texts, e.g. labelled diagrams, captions for pictures, to make class books, e.g. *What we know about . . . , Our Pets*	**64**						
22 to write own questions prior to reading for information and to record the answers, e.g. as lists, a completed chart, extended captions, for display, a fact file on IT	*57*						

Main learning outcome: to spell common words from Appendix List 1 (W9)

Further outcome: to read on sight high frequency words specific to graded reading books (W4)

Activity: Ask the children to read each sentence in turn and decide which word is missing. They then write it in the gap, trying to spell it without help. At the end of the activity, tell them to look in the book to see if they were right.

Further activity: Ask the children to make a list of all the words they know they can spell for themselves. Some children might want to restrict this by writing as many words with two letters as they can.

Main learning outcome: to predict text from the grammar, read on, leave a gap and re-read (S2)

Further outcome: to continue demarcating sentences in writing, ending a sentence with a full stop (S5)

Activity: Ask the children to read each sentence and decide which word is best to fill the gap. Tell them to write the word on the line. From memory or from the book, ask the children to add another sentence to answer the question 'What else did Kipper do?' and illustrate it.

Further activity: Ask the children to make up four more sentences using 'pulled', 'climbed', 'sat' and 'jumped'. They can write them on the back of the sheet.

Main learning outcome: to build simple profiles of characters from stories read (T15)

Further outcome: to apply phonological, graphic knowledge and sight vocabulary to spell words accurately (T12)

Activity: Ask the children what they know about Kipper. Read the first sentence with them. Ask them to make up three more sentences about Kipper. If there are words they cannot spell (e.g. 'brother') ask them to look in word books or have a try at spelling it.

Further activity: Ask the children to write on the back of the sheet about something that Kipper once did (e.g. making a cake, losing his teddy, having his hair cut).

Name ______________________ Date ______________

Write the missing words. Spell them yourself!

This house was .... sale.

Kipper looked .... the chimney.

Kipper climbed .... tree.

Write a word to fill the gap in these sentences:

Biff .... Chip climbed the tree.

.... went in the tree house.

Kipper pulled a can ....

Everyone .... the house.

Name ______________________ Date ____________   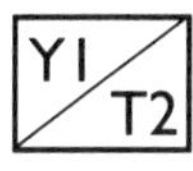

What did Kipper do?

Choose the right word for each sentence.

Kipper .... the wallpaper.

Kipper .... on the bed.

Kipper .... on a chair.

Kipper .... the tree.

pulled
climbed
sat
jumped

What else did Kipper do? Write one more sentence and draw the picture.

....

Work check

Name ____________________ Date ____________  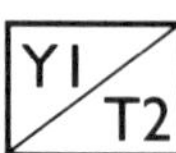

Write 3 more sentences about Kipper.

Kipper has a sister called Biff.

Work check

Main learning outcome: to make collections of words related to particular topics (W10)

Further outcome: to read on sight familiar words, e.g. equipment labels (W5)

Activity: Ask the children to read the words beneath the boxes and draw the pictures. Then tell them to use a picture dictionary, word banks, labels or their own spelling to write the words for other items of furniture or possessions that a family would put in a removal van. They can then draw the pictures.

Further activity: Ask the children to continue the list on the back of the sheet. They could use a CD rom picture dictionary for more ideas and to check spelling.

Main learning outcome: to use capital letters for names (S7)

Further outcome: to continue demarcating sentences in writing, ending with a full stop (S5)

Activity: Ask the children to scan the story of *The New House* to find out who said each sentence. Ask them to write the name or pronoun correctly and remind them of the full stop.

Further activity: Tell the children to look at page 6. What do they think the neighbours are saying? Ask them to write two sentences.

Main learning outcome: to represent outlines of story plots using captions and pictures (T14)

Further outcome: to use some of the elements of known stories to structure own writing (T16)

Activity: Ask the children to scan through the story of *The New House* to see what was put into the van. Then tell them to draw and write the names of four objects.

Further activities: Ask the children to write a story called *Moving House*. It could re-tell what happened in the story or be an account of the child's own family.

Name ______________________ Date ______________ IW Y1/T2

Read the words and draw the pictures.

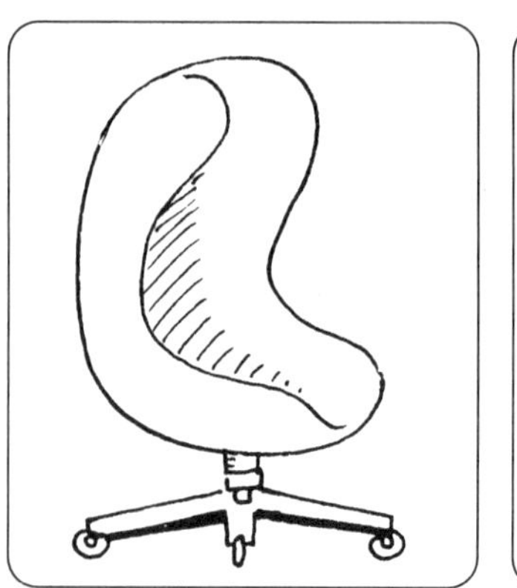

chair bed television go-kart

Draw 4 more things you take with you when you move house.

....

Use a picture dictionary to help you to write the words.

Work check

Name ______________________________ Date ______________ 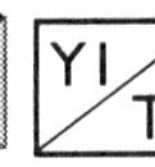

Look in the *The New House* to find the missing names.

'What a big van,' said .... page 2

'What a big man,' said .... page 3

'What a job,' said .... page 7

'What a big box,' said .... page 10

'What a job!' said .... page 11

'Come and play soon,' .... said. page 13

Look at page 6.
What do you think Mum said?

.... said Mum.

Work check

Name ______________________ Date ____________ 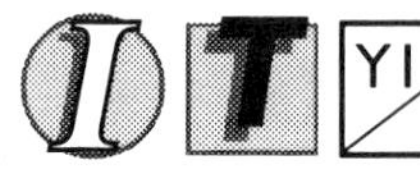

What did they put in the van?

Look in the book to find out.

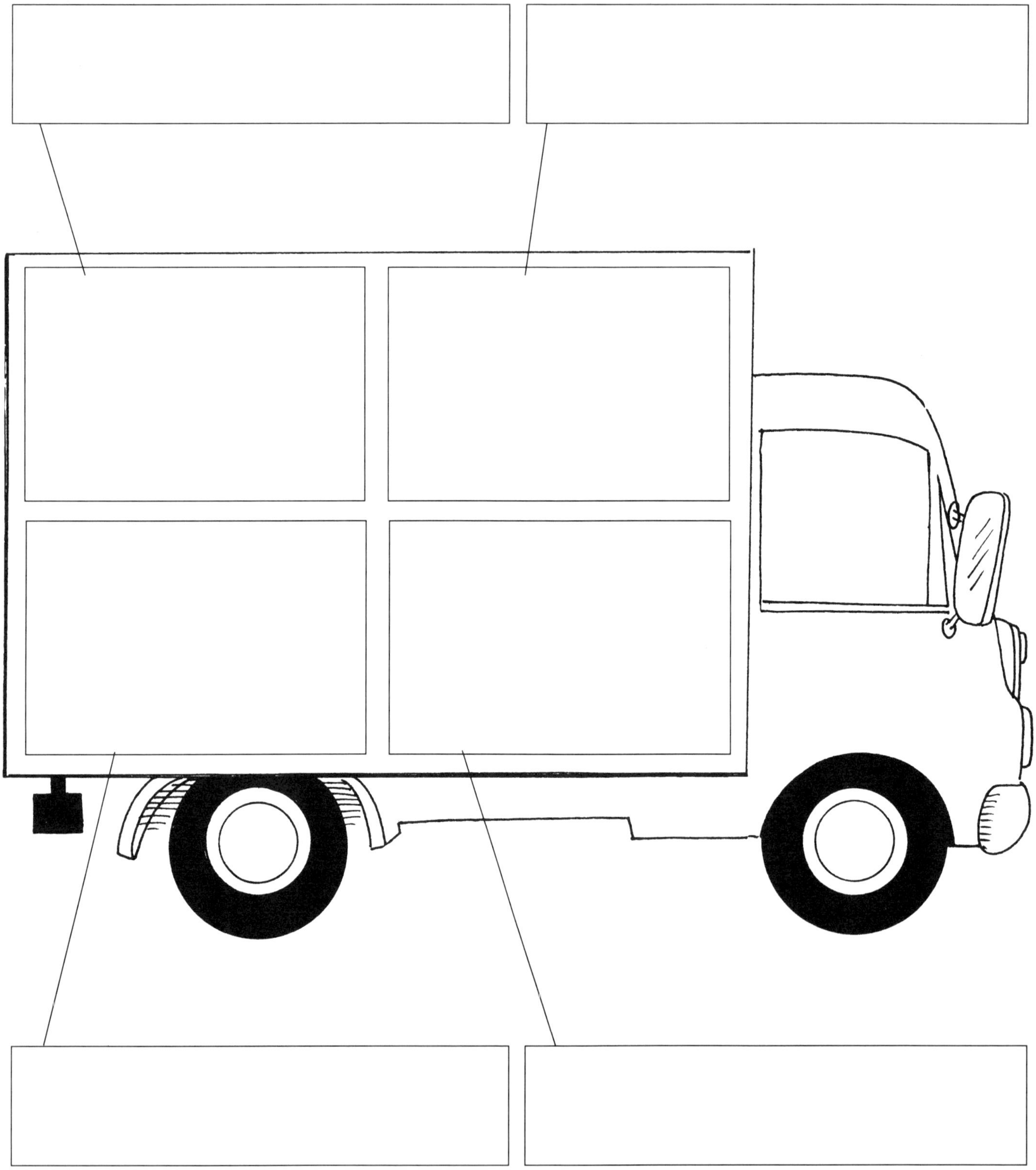

Draw the things in the van.

Write the words in the boxes.

Work check

Main learning outcome: to read on sight high frequency words from list – numbers one to ten (W6)

Further outcome: high frequency words – numbers one to twenty (W6)

Activity: Ask the children to use the text to find missing number words to match the pictures. Tell them to copy the number words and write the figures for numbers one to ten.

Further activity: Children could use a frieze or a dictionary to continue on the back of the sheet, writing number words to 20. Use the pattern in numbers to spell number words beyond 20.

Main learning outcome: to expect text to make sense and check for sense if it does not (S1)

Further outcome: to continue demarcating sentences in writing, ending with a full stop (S5). Use capital letters for names and for the start of a sentence (S7)

Activity: Ask the children to use one of the illustrated words to fill the gap in each sentence. Then, ask them to copy any two of the sentences, putting a different word at the end to make funny sentences.

Further activity: Children could write some more sentences on the back of the sheet. Ask them to change the beginning or end of other sentences, e.g. 'What a lot of biscuits!', 'Four children came to the door.', 'Dad was watching television.'

Main learning outcome: to re-tell stories, giving the main points in sequence (T4)

Further outcome: to apply phonological, graphic knowledge and sight vocabulary to spell words correctly (T12)

Activity: Ask the children to re-tell the story in *Come In!* including all the main points.

Further activities: Check through the story, underlining spellings the child is unsure about. Encourage the children to use dictionary word banks or word books to check and correct their own work.

Name ______________________ Date ______________ I W Y1/T2

How many children came to play?

.... children came to the house.

.... children came to the house.

.... children came to play.

Copy each word and write the numbers.

one	two	three	four	five
one	....	....	....	....
1				

six	seven	eight	nine	ten
....	....	....	....	....

Work check 

Name ______________________ Date ______________ 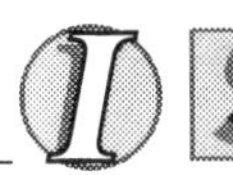 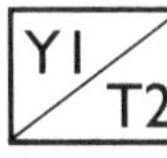

Choose the right word to finish each sentence.

Dad was painting the ....

house

Three children came to the ....

biscuits

They were watching ....

door

Mum gave the children some ....

television

Copy any two sentences and put the wrong word at the end to make a silly sentence.

Dad was painting the biscuits.

1 ....

2 ....

Work check 

Name ______________________ Date ____________  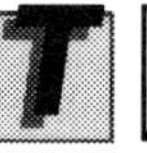 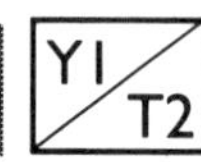

Can you remember the story?
Write what happened.

Dad was busy painting. Mum went out.

....

....

....

....

....

....

Draw a picture from your story.

Work check

Main learning outcome: to recognize the critical features of words, e.g. length (W7)

Further outcome: to read on sight high frequency words specific to graded reading books (W4)

Activity: Ask the children to look at the shape of words: the length, the letters with ascenders and those with descenders. Tell them to match each word to its shape, then write the letters in the boxes. Ask the children to look in the story book to find words to fit the last three shapes, and to write the words in the boxes. Remind them that letters with ascenders and descenders should fit into boxes of the right shape.

Further activity: On the back of the sheet, children could make a list of words from *The Secret Room* that have six or more letters. Then they could make a list of words with only two letters, from the book or other sources.

Main learning outcome: to predict words from preceding words in sentences and investigate the sorts of words that fit (S3)

Further outcome: to predict words from preceding words in sentences and investigate the sorts of words that fit, suggesting appropriate alternatives, i.e. that make sense (S3)

Activity: Ask the children to read the beginning of each sentence and then look in the box of sentence endings. Tell them to decide on the best way to finish each sentence. Ask them to write the end of the sentence on the line.

Further activity: Children could write the sentences again, but make up their own ending. For example, 'Biff opened the window.', 'Kipper found a key.' etc.

Main learning outcome: to present outlines of story plots using arrows to record the main incidents in order (T14)

Further outcome: to identify and record some key features of story language and to practise using them (T5)

Activity: Ask the children to read the sentences in the boxes. They must decide the correct order and show this by joining the boxes with arrows. Tell them to write the sentence to say what happened next.

Further activities: On the back of the sheet, ask the children to write a story about the three little children in the house starting, 'Once upon a time...'

Name ______________________ Date ______________ Y1/T2

Match each word to its shape.
Write the words in the shapes.

was

went

wanted

w a s

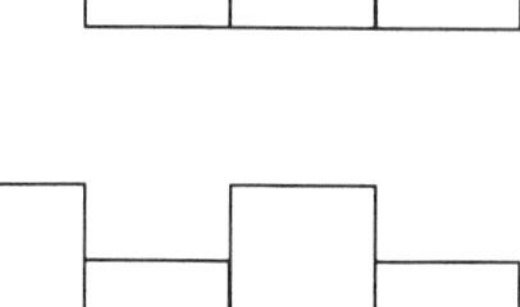

look

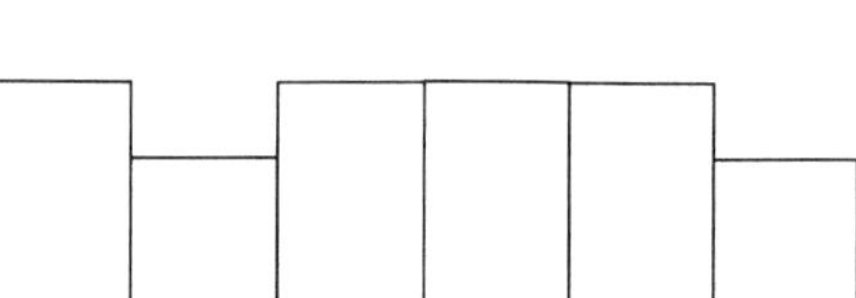

like

little

Find words in the book to fit these shapes:

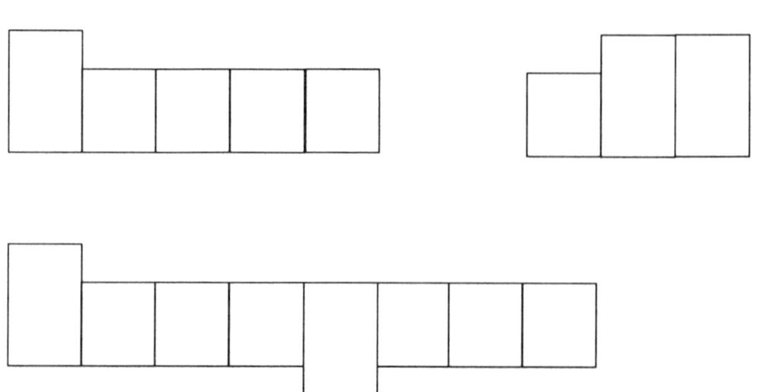

Work check

Name ______________________ Date ______________ I S Y1/T2

Choose the right ending to finish each sentence.

Biff opened the little house.

Kipper found a ....

Chip found ....

Biff was ....

Dad painted the ....

in bed.
secret room.
the little house.
three little children.
little dog.

Finish this sentence yourself:

Biff dreamed about ....

....

Work check

Name ______________________ Date ______________ 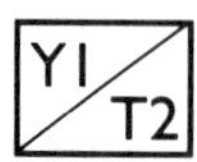

Draw arrows to tell the story in the right order.

Biff found a door.

Mum went into the secret room.

The door was stuck.

Mum opened the door.

She found a little house.

What happened next?

Write the sentence here.

....

....

Work check

Main learning outcome: to discriminate, read and spell words with initial consonant clusters (W3)

Further outcome: to identify separate phonemes in words containing clusters in speech and writing (W3)

Activity: Ask the children to read the words beginning with *gl*. Then tell them to look at the words in the word box beginning with *cl*, *fl* or *pl*. Explain that the children need to write each word in the right list. They could add more from a dictionary.

Further activity: Children could count the phonemes in each word in the box. Tell them to list them on the back of the sheet under headings:

3 phonemes	4 phonemes	5 phonemes	6 phonemes
f-l-y	p-l-u-s	f-l-ow-er-s	p-l-ay-t-i-me

Or they could make lists of words starting with *cr*, *fr* and *pr*. Suggest that they use a dictionary to help.

Main learning outcome: to use the term *sentence* appropriately (S6)

Further outcome: to expect reading to make sense and check for sense if it does not (S1); to use capital letters for the start of a sentence (S7)

Activity: Ask the children to read the words in each box. They need to decide how the sentence should begin and use all the words to make a sensible sentence. Remind them that the first word in the sentence must have a capital letter.

Further activity: Children could copy a sentence from the book on a strip of paper (remind them about a full stop), then cut it up into words. They could then ask a friend to make it into a sentence.

Main learning outcome: to use some of the elements of known stories to structure own writing (T16)

Further outcome: to apply phonological, graphic knowledge and sight vocabulary to spell words accurately (T12)

Activity: Ask the children to look at the book and talk about the wet playtime. Decide whether to write about the wet playtime in Mrs May's class or in your own class.

Further activities: Children could check their spelling using the story book, a dictionary, a word book or word lists. Ask them to draw two pictures on the back of the sheet to go with their story.

Name ______________________ Date ____________

Look in the word box.
Find and read the words
beginning with **gl**.
Write the **gl** words on the glider.

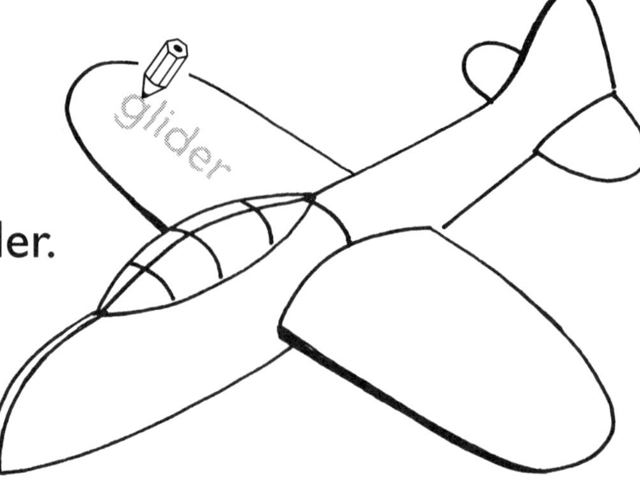

Word Box				
class	play	glass	flowers	climbed
playtime	flag	clock	glue	plus
flat	clap	glow	plan	fly

Write the other words in the right lists.

cl	fl	pl
class		

Work check

Name ______________________ Date ____________   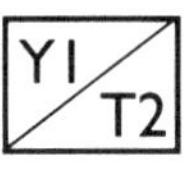

Sort out the words to make sentences.

school went Biff Chip and to .

Biff and Chip went to school.

liked Mrs May and Biff Chip .

. class They in her were

It time was story .

Look in the book. Draw story time here.

Work check

Name ______________________ Date ____________ 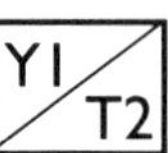

Write a story about the wet playtime in *The Play*, or
Write a story about a wet playtime at your school.

There was a storm. It was playtime. The children couldn't play outside.

....

....

....

....

....

....

....

....

Work check

Main learning outcome: to investigate, read and spell words ending in *ff, ll, ss, ck, ng* (W2)

Further outcome: to segment clusters into phonemes for spelling (W3)

Activity: Ask the children to look in the word box for more words ending in *ff* and to write them in Biff's box. Ask them to read the other words in the word box, then write them in the correct list.

Further activity: Explore further words ending in *ll* by thinking of words to rhyme with 'ill' and 'fell'. The children could write them in lists on the back of the sheet. Continue by finding words to rhyme with 'bang' and 'swing'.

Main learning outcome: to use capital letters for names (S7)

Further outcome: to continue demarcating sentences in writing, ending a sentence with a full stop (S5)

Activity: Ask the children to look at the beginning of the book to find the missing names. Then tell them to look near the end of the book to find out what Floppy did. Ask the children to write the sentence and draw the picture.

Further activity: The children could write three sentences about the storm. These can be found in the book if the children need help, e.g. 'The wind blew.', 'The rain came down.', 'The tree was down.'

Main learning outcome: to discuss reasons for, or causes of, incidents in stories (T7)

Further outcome: to retell stories, giving the main points in sequence (T4)

Activity: Ask the children to read the beginning of the first sentence and decide which ending makes sense. Encourage them to use the page references to help if necessary.

Further activities: Ask the children to explain how Floppy found the box. Where was it? How was it uncovered?

Name ______________________ Date ______________ Y1/T2

Biff has a box of words
ending in **ff**.
Look in the word box.
Find some more words ending with **ff**.
Write them in Biff's box.

Word Box
mess cliff wall thing going
cross bang puff ill less
swing ball fell cuff miss tell

Write the other words in the right list.

ss

ll

ng

Name ______________________ Date ______________ 

Who did it?

Look at the beginning of the book to find the answers.

[ ] helped the children.

[ ] and  mended the door.

[ ] painted the door.

[ ] painted the walls.

Now look at page 21. What did Floppy do?

Floppy ....

Draw the picture.

Work check 

Name ______________________ Date ____________  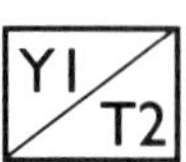

Look in the box to find the end of each sentence.

Biff was in her room because it was bedtime.

Wilf and Wilma came because ....

....

The mums and dads came because ....

....

Floppy barked and barked because ....

....

. . . it was bedtime. (page 10)
. . . he found something. (pages 20 and 21)
. . . it was time for school. (page 12)
. . . it was time to go home. (page 16)

Work check

Further text work to support teaching objectives from Y1T2

A book review (page 37)

Main learning outcomes: to choose and read familiar books; to discuss preferences and give reasons

Further outcome: to identify and discuss characters (T8)

Activity: Ask the children to choose any book they have read and write down the title, author and illustrator. Ask them to complete the sentences on the page and illustrate the sheet by copying the cover.

Further activity: Ask the children to list all the characters from the story on the back of the sheet and to say which is their favourite character.

Story themes (page 38)

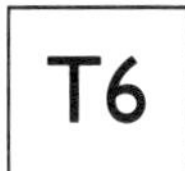

Main learning outcome: to identify and discuss a range of story themes, and to collect and compare

Activity: Ask the children to look back at familiar books and recall stories where Floppy gets into trouble. This could include books from any stage which are accessible in the classroom. Ask them to collect the books and copy the titles. Then ask them to make a list of the books in which Floppy is good.

Further activity: Ask the children to select their own theme and make a list on the back of the sheet, or ask them to list three stories when Dad gets cross.

How characters behave (page 39)

Main learning outcome: to identify and discuss characters; speculate about how they might behave

Activity: Ask the children to think about times when Mum has been cross with the children. Ask them to think of a different story where Mum would get cross: Who made a mess? or pulled something over? or ate all the cake?

Further activity: What would make Mum happy? Ask the children to write down two things that the characters could do to make Mum pleased with them.

Beginnings and endings (page 40)

Main learning outcome: to identify and compare basic story elements, e.g. beginnings and endings in different stories

Activity: Talk about *House For Sale* and what happens at the beginning of the story. Encourage the children to look in the book to check. Ask the children 'What happens at the end?' Again, look in the book to check. Ask the children to choose two other Stage 4 stories and finish the sentences on the sheet. They could work in pairs and help each other.

Further activity: Ask the children to think of a story they know well. It could be an *Oxford Reading Tree* story or a traditional story. Ask them to write one sentence about the beginning and one sentence about the end of the story. Ask other children to guess what it is. For example: Beginning – A girl goes into an empty house and eats the food on the table; End – She jumps out of the window and runs away. (The Three Bears)

Extending a poem (page 41)

Main learning outcome: to substitute and extend patterns from reading through language play

Activity: Read the poem **Thin and Fat** by John Foster from *Acorns* poetry, Size poems. Discuss opposites and ask the children to complete the suggestions and think of some more. Ask the children to choose a pair of opposites to make their own poem, e.g. rough things and smooth things, then make their own lists. Children may prefer to work in pairs and help each other, or work as a group with an adult.

Further activity: Choose a different pair of opposites and make another list poem.

Fiction or non-fiction? (page 42)

Main learning outcome: to use terms 'fiction' and 'non-fiction', noting some of their differing features.

Activity: Talk about the difference between 'fiction' and 'non-fiction'. How can you tell by looking at a book? Use a few books as examples. Are they fiction or not? How do you know? Provide a box of mixed books and ask children to choose three fiction and three non-fiction, copying the titles onto the covers drawn on the sheet.

Further activity: Children could exchange sheets with a friend. Tell the children to find the books listed and to tick the titles if they agree.

Dictionary practice (page 43)

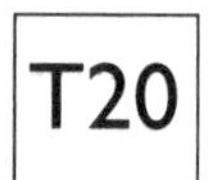

Main learning outcome: to use simple dictionaries and to understand their alphabetical organization

Activity: Choose a simple dictionary that includes definitions or sentences including each word. Help the children to find 'ambulance' and read what it says. Compare this with the definition on the sheet. Ask the children where they will look for 'apple' – at the beginning or at the end of the dictionary? Do they know why? Ask the children to continue finding the words illustrated and copying the definitions.

Further activity: Ask the children to find the first word listed for each of the next few letters of the alphabet, i.e. the first word in the dictionary beginning with 'e', 'f', 'g', etc.

Writing questions (page 44)

Main learning outcome: to write simple questions, e.g. as part of an interactive display

Activity: Ask the children the question already on the sheet. Explain that the other shapes are for more questions about books they have read. Show the children the question words at the bottom of the page. Remind them about question marks. You could give them a sheet each or enlarge the sheet and cut it up so that the children have one question each to write. These could be large enough to use in a display.

Further activity: Ask the children to make up more questions using question words they have not already used. They could include 'How?' and 'Why?'

Writing a simple report (page 45)

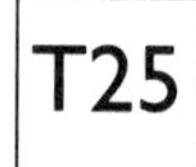

Main learning outcome: to assemble information from own experience; to write simple non-chronological accounts

Activity: Choose a topic of personal interest or related to class work. Ask the children to write the title of the report and finish the sentence about what they already know. Provide the children with a range of appropriate non-fiction books from which to select. Ask them to find one interesting fact they did not know before and write it down. Then ask them to write the title of the book they used.

Further activity: Ask the children to find out two more facts about their topic and write them on the back of the sheet.

Name ______________________ Date ______________  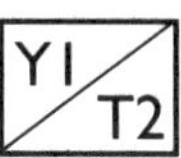

A book review

I have chosen ....

by ....

illustrated by ....

I like this book because

....

....

....

....

....

....

The best part is when ....

....

....

Work check

Name ______________________ Date ______________ A T Y1/T2

Look at books about Floppy.

Find 4 books where Floppy gets into trouble.

Write the titles on the covers.

Make a list of books where Floppy is good.

....

....

....

....

Work check

Name ______________________ Date ____________ 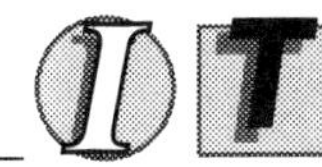 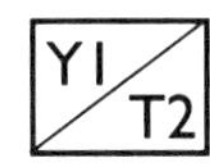

Who is this?

What makes her cross?

....

....

....

....

Make up a story where Mum gets cross.

....

....

....

....

....

....

....

Work check

T8 identify and discuss characters; speculate on how they might behave

Name ______________________ Date ______________ Y1/T2

Beginnings and endings

At the beginning of this story

At the end of this story

everyone likes the house.

At the beginning of this story

....

At the end of this story

....

At the beginning of this story

....

At the end of this story

....

Work check

T10 identify and compare beginnings and endings of different stories

Name ____________________ Date ______________ Y1 T2

Thin and fat by John Foster

(from *Acorns* poetry, Size poems)

Thin things:
A piece of cotton,
A bit of string,
A drinking straw,
A pencil,
A pin.

Fat things:
A huge tree trunk,
A hippo's belly,
An air balloon,
A giant jelly.

Make a list of opposites.

Big and .... and ....

Tall and .... and ....

.... and light .... and ....

Write your own poem, like 'Thin and fat'.

....

....

....

....

....

Work check

Name ______________________ Date ______________

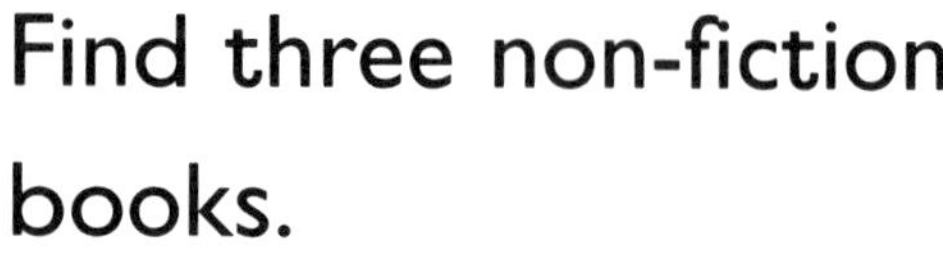

Find three fiction books.

Draw their covers here.

Find three non-fiction books.

Draw their covers here.

Work check

 T17 use the terms 'fiction' and 'non-fiction'

Name ______________________ Date ______________ Y1/T2

Find these words in your dictionary.
Write what the dictionary says.

ambulance

a van for taking injured or ill people to hospital.

apple

....

....

balloon

....

....

cat

....

....

dog

....

....

Name ______________________ Date ____________

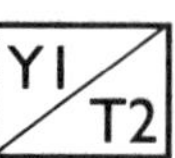

Choose any stories from stage 4.

Make up a quiz for other children to answer.

(Look in)

Who found a box under a tree?
(Look in *The Storm.*)

(Look in)

(Look in)

Question words:

(Look in)

Who? When? What? Where?

Work check

T24 to write simple questions, e.g. as part of an interactive display

Name ______________________ Date ______________  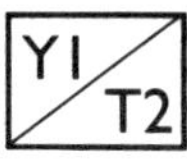

I want to find out about ....

....

I already know that ....

....

The best thing I have found out is that ....

....

....

....

This book helped me.

Work check

Assessment Y1T2

Three phonemes in simple words (page 48)

Objective: Can the child identify, read and write initial, medial and final sounds in simple words?

Activity: Ask the child to trace over the lines linking 'b-u-n', saying the sounds as he or she does so. Ask him or her to show you how to make other words in the same way, by drawing mapping lines linking the letters. Ask the child to write their word on one of the lines on the side. Does the child read each word correctly? Has s/he used all the vowels and read them correctly? Has s/he made only words that are real words, or linked letters at random? Note and date your observations on the back of the sheet.

Three phonemes including 'two letters – one sound' (page 49)

Objective: Can the child read and spell words ending in *ff, ll, ss, ck ng?*

Activity: Ask the child to trace over the lines and read the word 'long' already on the page. Ask him or her to show you how another word could be made in the same way. Say that you want him or her to find as many words as possible in the same way, adding each word to the list and using the extra spaces if they can. When the child has finished, ask him or her to read all the words to you. Has s/he used all the double letter endings at least once? Has s/he read and spelled all the words correctly? Ask him or her to spell a few of the words for you without seeing the paper. Can s/he remember the endings? Note and date your observations on the back of the sheet.

Initial consonant clusters (page 50)

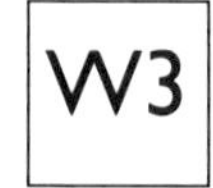

Objective: Can the child discriminate, read and spell words with initial consonant clusters?

Activity: Ask the child to trace over the lines and read the word 'from' already on the page. Ask him or her to show you how another word could be made in the same way. Say that you want him or her to find as many words as possible in the same way, adding each word to the list and using the extra spaces if they can. When the child has finished, ask him or her to read all the words to you. Has s/he used all the letter blends at least once? Has s/he read all the words correctly? Ask him or her to spell a few of the words for you without seeing the paper. Can s/he remember the blends? Note and date your observations on the back of the sheet.

Final consonant clusters (page 51)

Objective: Can the child discriminate, read and spell words with final consonant clusters?

Activity: Ask the child to trace over the lines and read the word 'sink' already on the page. Ask him or her to show you how another word could be made in the same way. Say that you want him or her to find as many words as possible in the same way, adding each word to the list and using the extra spaces if they can. When the child has finished, ask him or her to read all the words to you. Has s/he used all the letter blends at least once? Has s/he read all the words correctly? Ask him or her to spell a few of the words for you without seeing the paper. Can s/he remember the blends? Note and date your observations on the back of the sheet.

Stage 4 Key words (page 52)

Objective: Can the child read on sight high frequency words in Stage 4?

Activity: Ask the child to read the list of words to you. Tick all the words s/he can read accurately. Ask the child to use a colour to ring those words. If s/he uses the same colour, the next time the child reads the list and uses a different colour it will be clear to him or her how many more words have been learned. While the child is reading notice: Is the child reading the words confidently on sight? Is s/he using phonics to read the words? Is s/he using the first letter and guessing? If you note and date your observations on the back of the sheet this will help you provide targeted support during guided reading sessions and practice at home.

Assessing text level work

Any of the text level sheets could be used to assess reading comprehension or writing composition. Copymasters on pages 37, 42, 44 and 45 (book review, sorting fiction and non-fiction, making up questions and writing a simple report) are general activities which can be used more than once with the same child and used to assess those objectives.

Name ____________________ Date ____________

Y1/T2

How many words can you make?

b d

a

c g

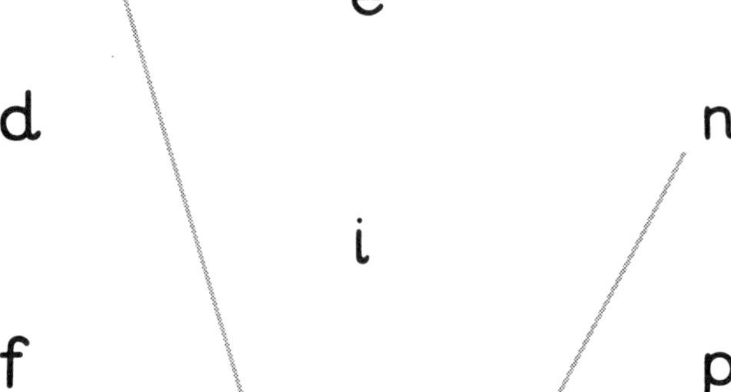

e

d n

i

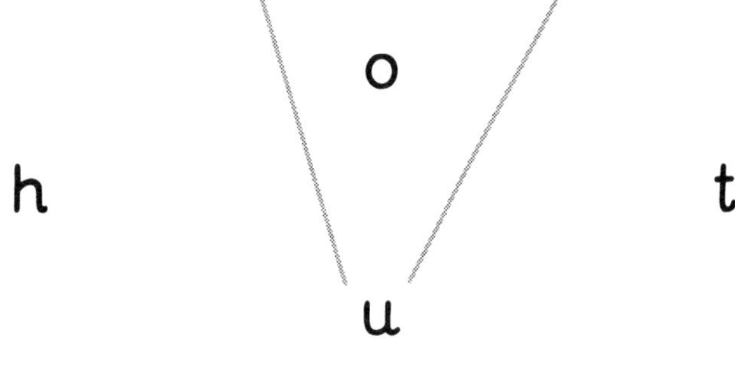

f p

o

h t

u

j w

Find some more words and write them here.

Work check

W1 secure identification, spelling and reading of initial, final and medial sounds in simple words

How many words can you make?

ch		ck	....
	a		....
k		ff	....
	e		....
l		ng	long
	i		....
qu		ll	....
	o		....
r		ss	....
	u		....
w		sh	....

Find some more words and write them here.

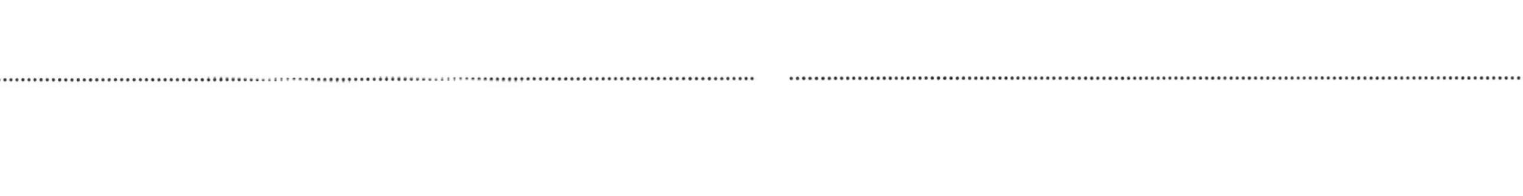

Work check

Name ______________________ Date ______________ IW Y1/T2

How many words can you make?

dr		g	....
	a		....
fl		m	from ....
	e		....
fr		n	....
	i		....
scr		p	....
	o		....
sk		sh	....
	u		....
sl		t	....

Make some more words and write them here.

....

....

....

Work check

 W3 to spell words with initial consonant clusters

Name ______________________ Date ______________ 

How many words can you make?

b		nd	....
	a		....
d		lk	....
	e		....
h		nk	sink
	i		....
l		mp	....
	o		....
s		nt	....
	u		....
th		st	....

Make some more words and write them here.

....

....

....

Work check

Name ______________________ Date ______________

Draw a coloured ring around the words you know.

for liked house this room

helped big things man

came Come play with door

painted little wallpaper found opened

There outside inside her him

mended time key storm box

Main learning outcome: to recognize words by common spelling patterns (W5)

Further outcome: to segment words into phonemes for spelling (W1)

Activity: Point out to the children that longer words that rhyme often share spelling patterns. Begin with 'Kipper' and 'slipper' and ask the children to try to spell both words, using the book if necessary. Then ask them to use the letters in the box to make new words to rhyme with the words in the list.

Further activity: Ask the children to list more words to rhyme with 'pin', 'book' and 'picked' using any letters or blends to start the word.

Main learning outcome: to expect reading to make sense and check for sense if it does not (S1)

Further outcome: to use awareness of grammar to predict text (S2)

Activity: Read the first sentence with the children and identify the mistake. Read the second sentence to show that the mistake has been corrected. Ask the children to read the remaining sentences and decide which word needs to be changed each time. Use the new words from the box to help with ideas and spelling.

Further activity: On the back of the sheet ask the children to write three sentences from the story, but leaving out one word in each sentence. Children could then pass the page to a friend and ask her or him to write the word that fits in the gap.

Main learning outcome: to write about significant incidents from known stories (T13)

Further outcome: to apply phonological, graphic knowledge and sight vocabulary to spell words accurately (T12)

Activity: Talk about the mouse in the story. Why were the children frightened? Ask the pupils to re-write the story, explaining why everything looked big.

Further activity: Encourage the children to read through their story, underlining any spellings they are not sure about. Ask them to have another try at spelling them or look in a dictionary, a word bank or word book to check them.

Name ________________________ Date ____________  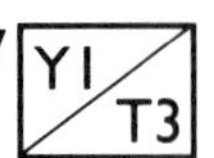

More rhyming words

rhymes with

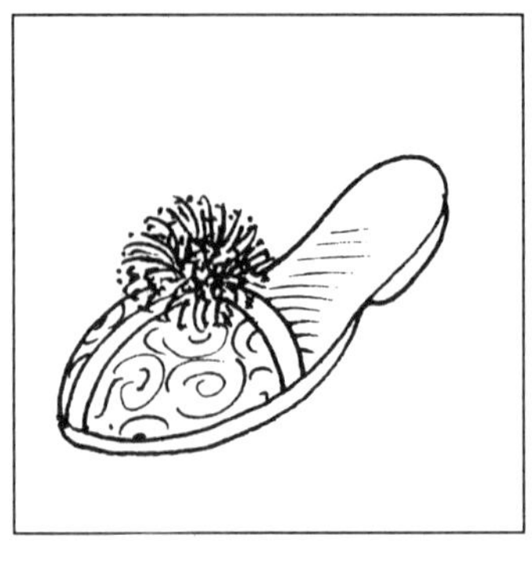

K..................................... ....

Use the letters in the box to make more rhymes.

pin	rhymes with	[ ]		b
box	———→	[ ]		c
book	———→	[ ]		f
house	———→	[ ]		k
picked	———→	[ ]		l
				m
				p
				t

Now make words to rhyme with:

glowing [ ] door [ ]

smaller [ ] looked [ ]

Work check

Name ______________________ Date ______________   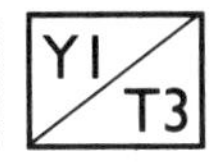

Each sentence has a mistake.
Write the correct sentence
using a word from the box.

They
was
went
at
looked
couldn't
went

1 The box wanted by Chip's bed.

The box was by Chip's bed.

2 Chip looked and the box.

....

3 Everything liked big.

....

4 Biff was to the door.

....

5 The went to the window.

....

Write the missing word in this sentence.

Chip pulled and pulled but he

.... get in.

Work check

Name ______________________ Date ____________  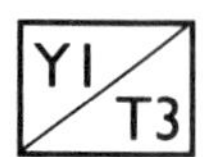

Biff and Chip met a mouse in this story.
Write the story of:

Biff, Chip and the mouse

....

....

....

....

....

....

....

....

....

....

....

Work check

Main learning outcome: to know the terms 'vowel' and 'consonant' (W9)

Further outcome: to segment words into phonemes for spelling (W1)

Activity: Remind the children which letters are vowels. Read them on the sheet.
Show them where the consonants are listed. Say the names of the letters with the children. Ask them to look at the word 'pirates' and notice that the vowels have been separated into a box. Ask them which letters will go in the other box. Explain that they need to sort out the vowels and consonants for the three other words in boxes. Ask them to make words from the vowels and consonants listed at the bottom of the page.

Further activity: Ask the children to copy the vowels and consonants from the word 'adventure' onto the back of the sheet. Ask them to see how many words they can make from these letters.

Main learning outcome: to reinforce knowledge of the term 'sentence' (S6)

Further outcome: to add question marks to questions (S7)

Activity: Read the first question and answer with the children. Show them that the page numbers listed tell them where to find the answer to the questions. Make sure that they understand that a whole sentence is required for the answer.

Further activity: Children could look at pages 12 and 13 and make up some questions in the same way. Remind them to use question marks.

Main learning outcome: to recognize an ordered sequence of events using words like 'first', 'then', 'next' (T18)

Further outcome: to write own questions (T22)

Activity: Explain to the children that all the sentences they need to tell the story are in the box, but they have to decide on the order. When they copy the sentences the children should make sure that they copy sentences accurately and use their best handwriting.

Further activities: On the back of the sheet, ask children to make up their own story quiz for *Pirate Adventure.* Questions could be about the pictures, e.g. 'What colour is Wilf's shirt?', 'How many palm trees are there on page 11?'

Name ______________________ Date ____________ Y1/T3

These letters are vowels: a e i o u

These letters are consonants:

b c d f g h j k l m n p q r s t v w x y z

Sort out the letters in each word into vowels and consonants.

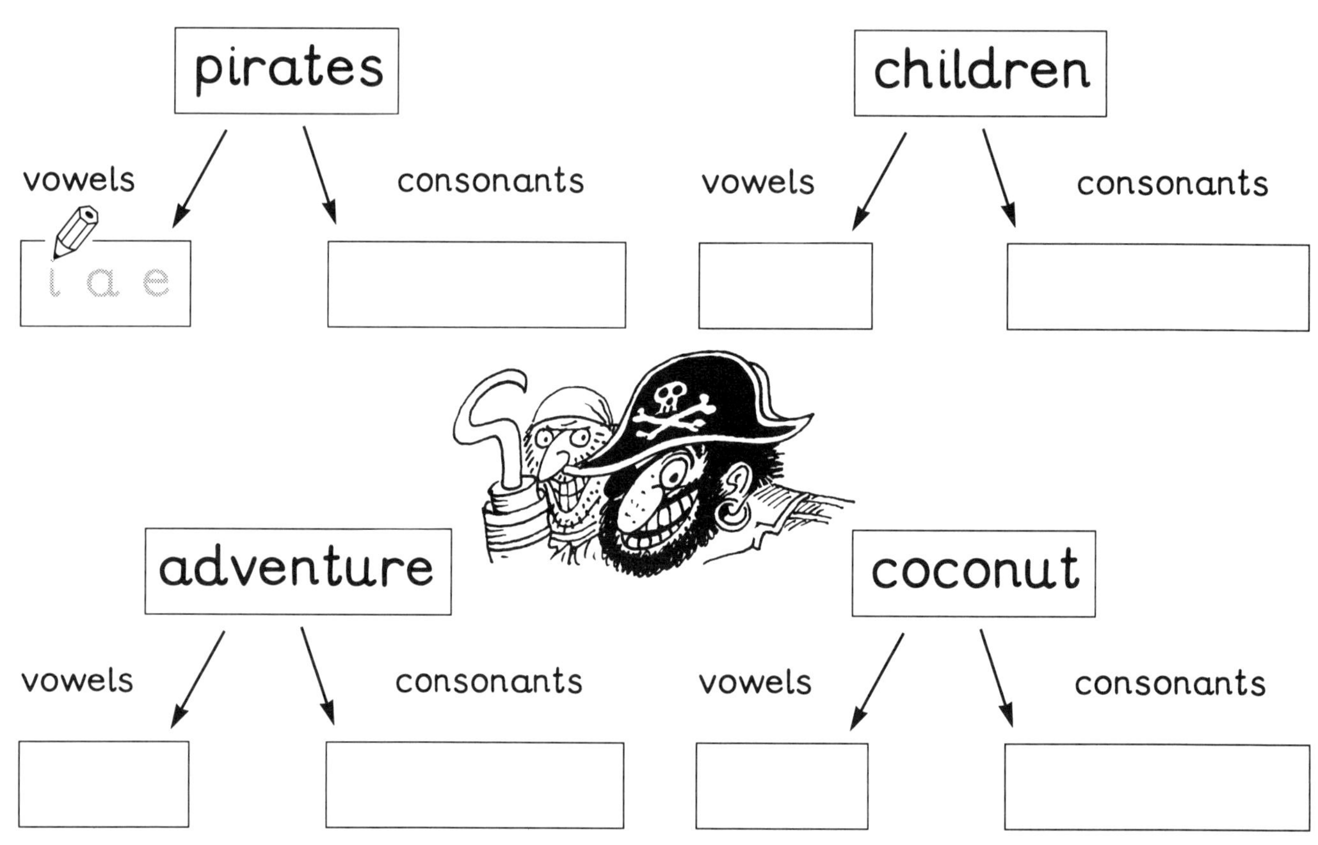

Make at least 5 words from these vowels: a e i
and these consonants: t p s l r .

Work check

Name ______________________ Date ______________  Y1/T3

Answer the questions.

Write a sentence each time.

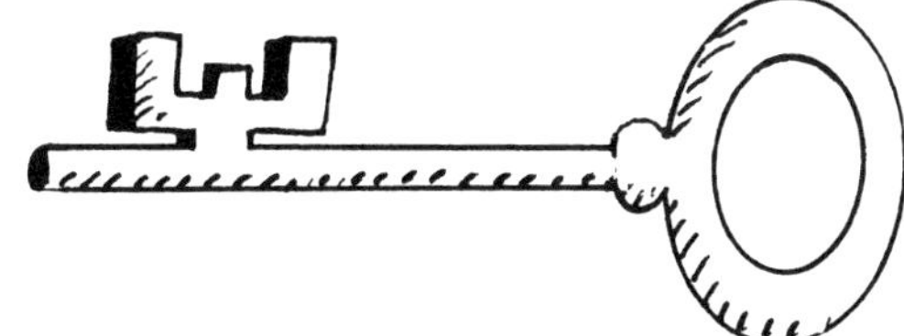

1 What began to glow? (page 5)

The key began to glow.

2 Who went inside the house? (page 10)

....

3 Who went in the sea? (page 13)

....

4 Who had a boat? (page 17)

....

5 Who wanted a party? (page 19)

....

Write another question and the answer.

Question: ....

Answer: ....

Work check

Name ______________________ Date ______________ 

Use the sentences in the box to tell the story in order.

. . . they went to the pirate ship

. . . they ran to the sea.

. . . a pirate came up.

. . . the children went to the party.

. . . it was time to go.

. . . the children went inside the house.

Pirate Adventure

First of all the children went inside the house.

Then ....

Suddenly ....

After that ....

Next, ...

At last ....

Work check

Main learning outcome: to know common spelling patterns for long vowel phoneme *ee* (W1)

Further outcome: to know common spelling patterns for the long vowel phoneme *ai* (W1)

Activity: Ask the children to look at the words in the word box and notice whether they have *ee* or *ea* to make the 'ee' sound. Discuss where 'sea' should be written and ask the children to copy it in the right place.

Further activity: Children could make lists of words to rhyme with 'tail', 'away' and 'make' on the back of the sheet.

Main learning outcome: to predict words from previous text (S4)

Further outcome: through reading and writing to reinforce knowledge of the term 'sentence' (S6)

Activity: Ask the children to read each sentence and to decide which of the three words fits best. If an adult is available, encourage the children to explain their choice.

Further activity: Children could write each sentence in turn on the back of the sheet, changing another word in the sentence, e.g. 'A robin flew out of a tree.' Remind the children to use a capital letter at the beginning of the sentence and a full stop at the end.

Main learning outcome: to use labelled diagrams to show 'What we know about . . . ' (T21)

Further outcome: to write stories using simple settings (T14)

Activity: Ask the children to write a sentence at the end of each labelling line to describe dragons in general. Point out the use of the present tense.

Further activities: Children could make up a story about meeting a dragon and tell how they escaped. They could write the story on the back of the sheet.

Name ______________________ Date ______________ Y1/T3

These phonemes say 'ee' in words:

ee in tr**ee** **ea** in s**ea**t **ey** in k**ey**

Write **ee** words on the tree.

Write **ea** words on the seat.

sea bee tea meat feet
treat three beef bean been
keep heating freezer leaf

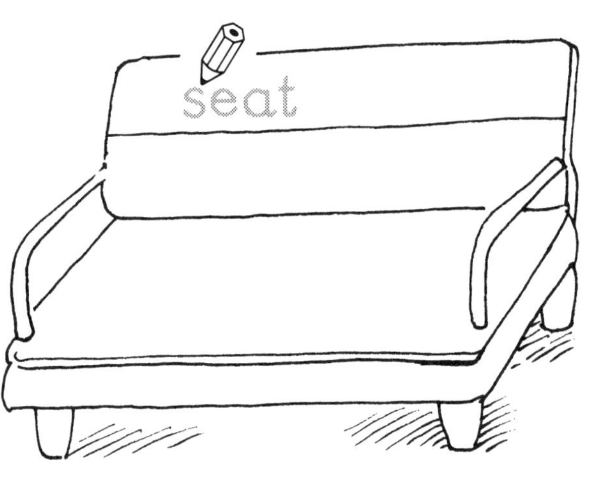

Write 'key' inside the key at least 6 times.

Use your best handwriting.

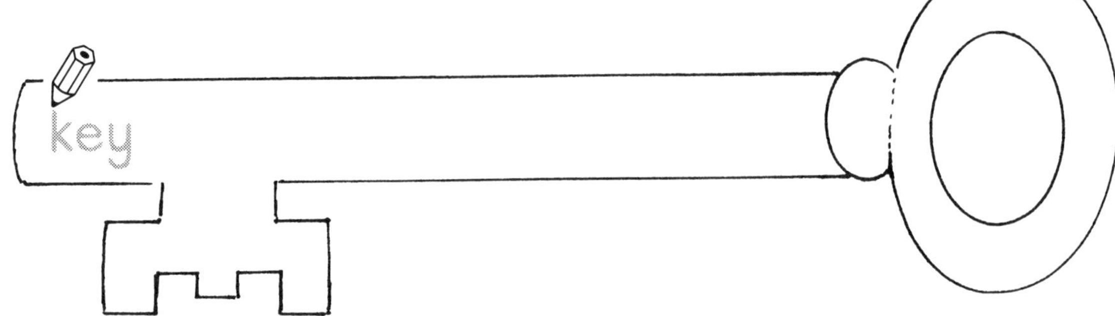

Work check

Name ______________________ Date ______________  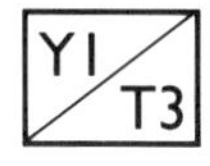

Choose the best word to fit in each sentence.

An owl flew out of a tree.

wood
tree
house

Floppy didn't .... the owl.

look
liked
like

.... ran away.

He
Her
Has

Floppy ran out .... the wood.

over
out
of

It was .... good.

no
one
on

Sort out the words in this sentence.

dragon the under tree A lived

....

Work check

Name ______________________ Date ______________ YI/T3

Write sentences to label this drawing.

What I know about dragons.

Dragons can breathe fire.

Work check

Main learning outcome: to investigate and learn spellings of verbs with 'ed' (past tense) and 'ing' (present tense) endings (W6)

Activity: Ask the children to read each sentence and choose the correct word from the three versions of the verb. Which one sounds right? Which one makes sense?

Further activity: The children could investigate verb patterns by sorting out the words in boxes on the sheet into two sets: one set where the verbs follow the pattern of play, playing, played and one set where there are differences, as in make, making, made. They could find more words from the book to add to their lists, e.g. 'yell', 'want', 'say', 'run', 'glow'.

Main learning outcome: other common uses of capitalization (S5)

Further outcome: to apply phonological, graphic knowledge and sight vocabulary to spell words accurately (T12)

Activity: Ask the children to look at the pages referred to on the sheet and to copy the wording from the notices using capital letters. They can then copy the other notices on to the boards drawn using capital letters. Encourage the children to keep their letters the same size, like a real notice.

Further activity: The children could think of a useful notice for their classroom, such as 'Please close the door', or 'Please use our books carefully'. Encourage them to try out the spelling first, then copy in neat capital letters.

Main learning outcome: to use the title, cover pages, pictures and 'blurbs' to predict the content of familiar stories (T7)

Further outcome: to apply phonological, graphic knowledge and sight vocabulary to spell words accurately (T12)

Activity: Ask the children to write the title and author on the front cover of the outline. Tell them to think of a new incident when Gran gets into trouble, e.g. at the supermarket or on the bus. Who gets cross with her? Encourage the children not to tell the whole story, just write some clues about what happens. Then they could draw a picture on the front of the cover to illustrate their idea.

Further activities: The children could swap covers, then read about Gran's problem and write the whole story from the beginning, deciding how it will end. Put the stories inside the covers and keep them in the reading corner for everyone to read.

Name ______________________ Date ______________ IW Y1/T3

Choose the right word for each sentence.

1	Gran came to .... with the children.	play playing played
2	Gran .... the children.	like liking liked
3	They went on the .... castle.	jump jumping jumped
4	'Come on, Gran', they	call calling called
5	Gran .... a hole in the castle.	make making made
6	The castle began to .... down.	go going went
7	'.................. at my castle,' yelled the man.	Look Looking Looked
8	Gran .... the children home.	take taking took

Name ______________________ Date ______________ 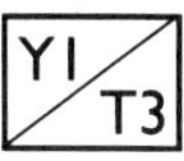

NOTICES often use capital letters.

Find these notices and copy them in capital letters.

page 12 page 19

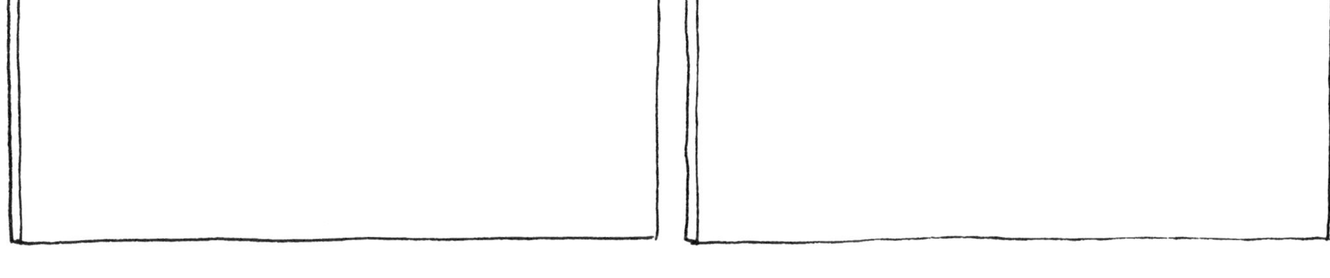

Use capital letters to write these notices.

no parking please keep off the grass

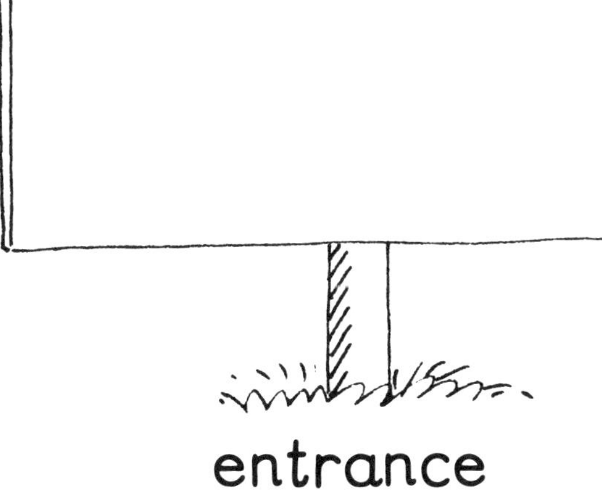

entrance way out

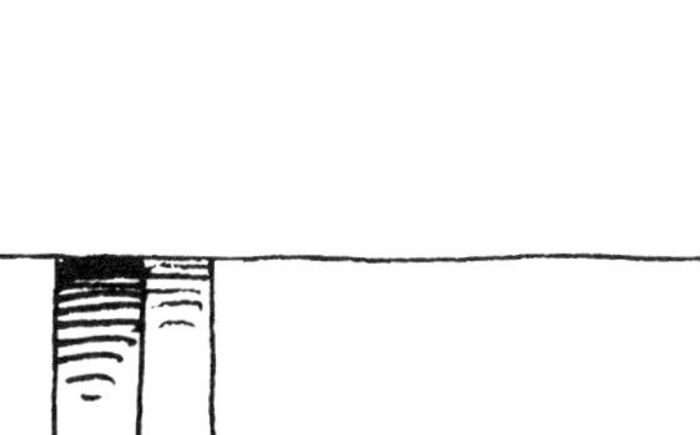

Name ______________________ Date ______________ 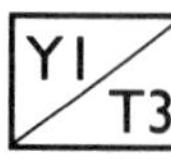

Make the cover for a story called:

Gran in trouble!

Fold

Gran gets into trouble when

Main learning outcome: to read on sight common colour words, Appendix List 1 (W4)

Further outcome: to make collections of words related to particular topics (W8)

Activity: Ask the children to read the captions and draw and colour the right witch in each space. Then ask them to read the colour words and colour the stars correctly. Encourage the children to look in a dictionary, in word books, word banks or on coloured pencils or crayons to find six more colour words. Ask the pupils to copy the words and colour the stars appropriately.

Further activity: On the back of the sheet, the children could write the alphabet, leaving space beside each letter. Ask them to write a colour word beside as many letters of the alphabet as possible. Encourage them to share ideas.

Main learning outcome: to add question marks to questions (S7)

Further outcome: to spell high frequency words from Appendix List 1 (focus on words for questions) (W7)

Activity: Ask the children to read the words in the speech bubbles. They must decide which ones are questions and add question marks. Ask them to use mapping lines to match each question to the right answer. Remind them to add a full stop to a statement.

Further activity: Children could make up one question for each of the question words Who? Why? Where? When? Which? How? For example, 'How did Gran catch a witch?', 'Why did she put the book on the fire?'

Main learning outcome: to compose carefully selected sentences (T16)

Further outcome: to use words like 'first', 'next', 'after' (T18)

Activity: Talk about the kinds of words that sound best in spells. Use some of the suggestions to decide what sounds best. Ask the children to list the ingredients for a spell for turning witches into frogs using some of the words suggested. Ask them to add more ingredients of their own.

Further activities: Children could write instructions to tell someone how to make the spell using 'First', 'Next', 'After that', to write the instructions in order. For example, 'First collect the berries and chop them up. Then . . . Next . . .'

Name ______________________ Date ____________

Draw and colour the three witches.

the green witch the red witch the black witch

Copy the colour words and colour the shapes.

blue yellow  brown 

....

Find some more colour words.

Write the words and colour the stars.

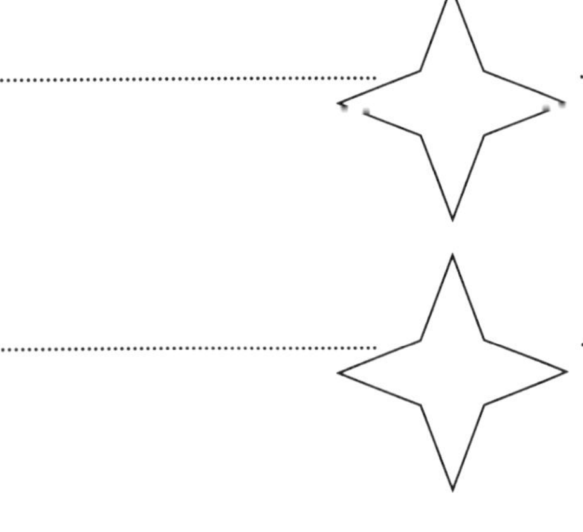

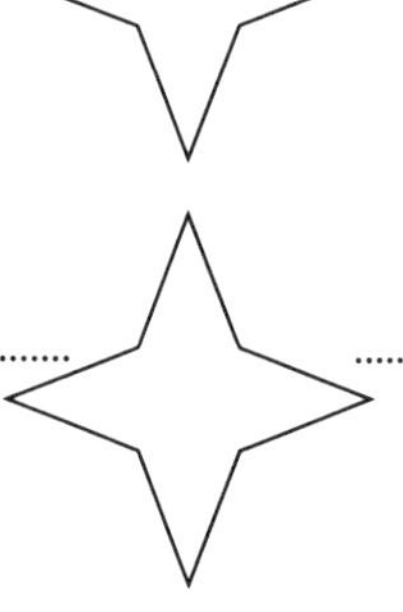

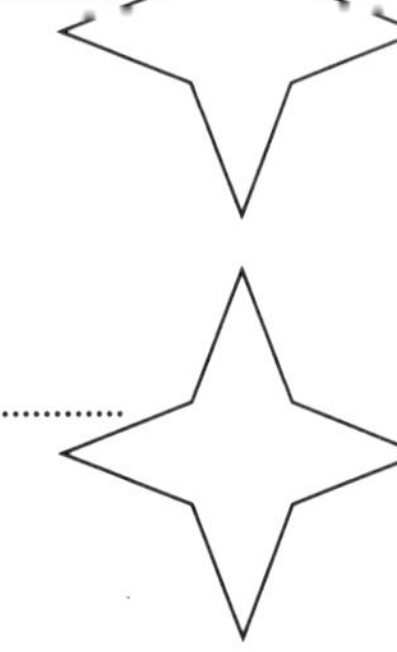

Work check

Name ______________________ Date ______________

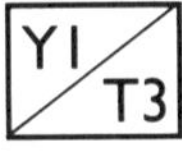

Add question marks to the questions.

Match the questions to the answers.

Who turned you into a frog?

The witches turned me into a frog.

Who put a net over the witch

The frogs turned into people.

What turned into people

Gran put a net over the witch.

The king had a party.

Who took the witch's keys

Chip took the witch's keys.

Who had a party

Write the question for this answer:

Biff and Gran looked in the witch's book.

Name ______________________ Date ______________  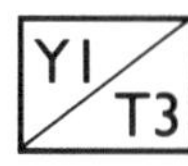

Make a spell to change witches into frogs.

Here are some ideas.

frogs-spawn plant

icicles

melted, frozen, crushed, blue

witch's hair

white, grey, tangled, knotted

How many of each do you need?

A handful? A hundred? A spoonful?

Write the things you need for your spell here.

Work check

Main learning outcome: to know the common spelling patterns for long vowel phonemes *oa* as in 'boat', *o-e* as in 'pole', *ow* as in 'show', Appendix List 3 (W1)

Further outcome: to know the common spelling patterns for long vowel sound *ie* as in 'lie', *i-e* as in 'bite', *igh* as in 'high', *y* as in 'fly' (W1)

Activity: Ask the children to read 'coat', 'glow' and 'home'. Point out that the 'o' has a long sound. Tell the children to read the words in the large O and decide where each one belongs. They must write each word in the set with the same spelling pattern. Remind them to check that they have used all the words.

Further activity: Children could write 'lie', 'nine', 'night', and 'fly' along the top of the other side of the sheet. Ask them to write at least two words to rhyme with each of them, using the same spelling pattern as the word at the top of the list.

Main learning outcome: to predict text from the grammar (S2)

Further outcome: to reinforce knowledge of the term 'sentence' (S6)

Activity: Read the extract from the text with the children. Ask them to read the words on the toboggan and decide which one makes sense. They should write the missing word in the gap. Encourage them to read the whole story to check that it makes sense. Tell them to look at pages 10–13 to find out what the book said. Reassure them that their story is still right if it makes sense.

Further activity: Children could choose three sentences from the book to copy out onto the back of the sheet, but ask them to leave out one word in each sentence. Tell them to find a partner who can write the missing word without looking in the book. They can then check for sense.

Main learning outcome: to re-tell stories, to give the main points in sequence and to pick out significant incidents (T5)

Further outcome: to identify simple questions and use the text to find answers (T19)

Activity: Read the beginning of the story with the children. Ask them to continue by writing what happened next. They may turn over and continue the story on the back of the sheet.

Further activities: Children to work with a friend to make up a quiz about the book using 'What?', 'Who?', 'Where?' to start their questions. Answers could be given verbally.

Name ______________________ Date ______________ IW Y1/T3

These phonemes say ‘o’ in words:

oa in c**oa**t **ow** in gl**ow** **o-e** in h**o**m**e**

Choose words from the O.

Write **oa** words on the coat.

Write **ow** words on the b**ow**.

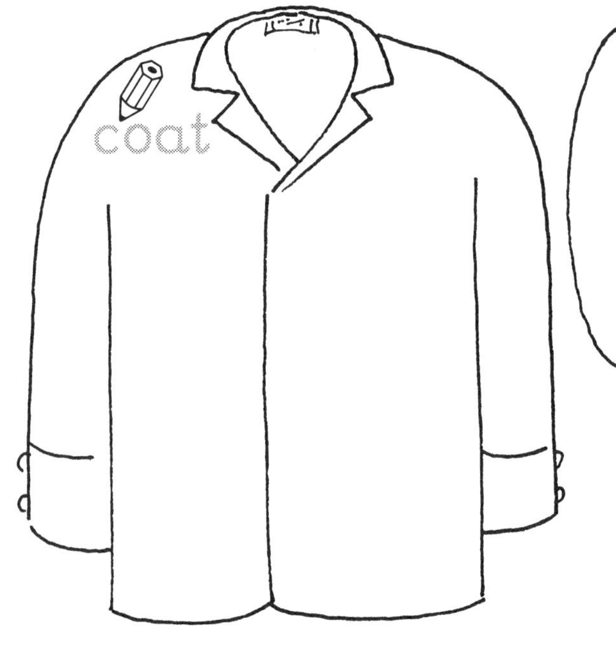

bow

Write **o-e** words on the bone.

bone

soap low hope
joke mole float
snow cone row
own goal goat
phone mow loaf
boat show oak
crow

Work check

Name ____________________ Date ______________  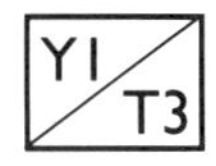

Read this story.
Choose a word from the toboggan that would fit in the gap.

Some big boys ran .... They pushed the little boy .... They .... the toboggan over and they ran .... The children .... up. They helped the .... boy. Kipper picked .... his hat. The little boy told them .... the big boys. Kipper .... cross.

up on in over off
away of was to little
big ran saw about put
came pushed pulled put

Name ______________________ Date ______________ YI/T3

What happened next?

Write the rest of the story.

Village in the snow

The boy was pulling a toboggan. Some big boys ran up. They pushed the little boy over.

....

....

....

....

Draw a picture from your story.

Work check

Practice with ai and a-e spellings (page 78)

Main learning outcome: to recognize long vowel sounds *ai* and *a-e* in words

Activity: Ask the children to look at the pictures of the train and the crane. Point out the different spellings of the two words. Ask the children to sort out the words in the box by writing them on the train or on the crane.

Further activity: Ask the children to make a list of words with *ai*, *a-e* or *ay* spelling patterns. They could look in books to help them.

Handwriting practice guidelines (page 79)

Main learning outcome: to practise hand writing in conjunction with spelling and independent writing, ensuring correct letter orientation, formation and proportion.

Activity: This sheet could be used for copying a poem or piece of writing, or for practising spelling patterns. The guidelines are intended to help children write with clear ascenders and descenders. The sheet could also be used behind plain paper as guidelines.

Compare story settings (page 80)

Main learning outcome: to compare and contrast stories with a variety of settings.

Activity: Collect a copy of each story, 1–6, at Stage 5. Ask the children to tell you briefly what happens in each story. Can they think of a way to sort the stories into two sets? If they find this difficult, ask 'Which stories are magic adventures?', 'What happens in the other stories?' Which do they prefer – magic stories or stories at home? Are magic stories more exciting? are 'home' stories funnier? Ask the children to choose one story about home or school and one magic adventure. Show them where to draw the cover of each and where to finish writing the sentence, 'I like this story because . . .' Then ask the children to decide which of the two books they prefer and give their reason.

Comparing a story with a poem (page 81)

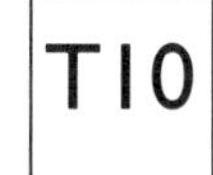

Main learning objective: to compare and contrast common themes in stories and poems.

Activity: Read the poem with the children. What does the girl think about playtime? Does she enjoy it? What happens at playtime in *The Play*? Do the children enjoy their playtime? Why? What is the same about the poem and the story? What is different? Ask the children to finish the sentences on the sheet in their own words.

Using poems as models for their own writing (page 82)

Main learning objective: to use poems or parts of poems as models for their own writing.

Activity: Read the poem with the children. Ask them to suggest names of other footwear to add to the list. Then ask them to think about what those shoes do. Add these words to the second list. Ask them to write verse two by starting with four more shoes and what they do. Don't worry about rhyming, although children might notice that 'slide' and 'glide' rhyme. The last four lines could be repeated.

Further activity: The children could learn the new poem by heart and present it to the class.

Name ______________________ Date ______________

On the train or on the crane?

Practise writing the words with the same spelling pattern on the right picture.

train	crane	brain
lane	rain	chain
cane	again	mane
pain	vane	stain
pane	main	drain

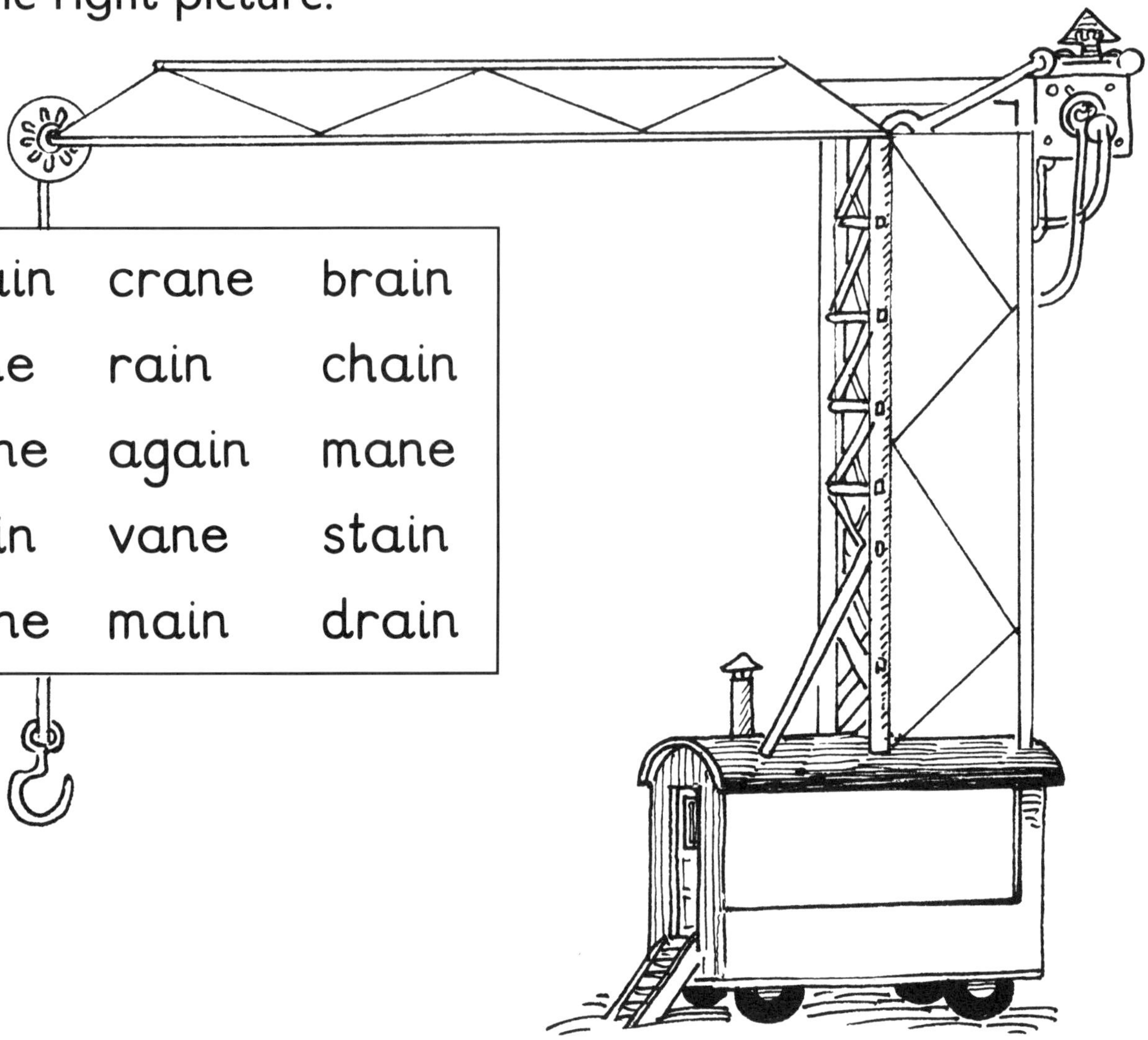

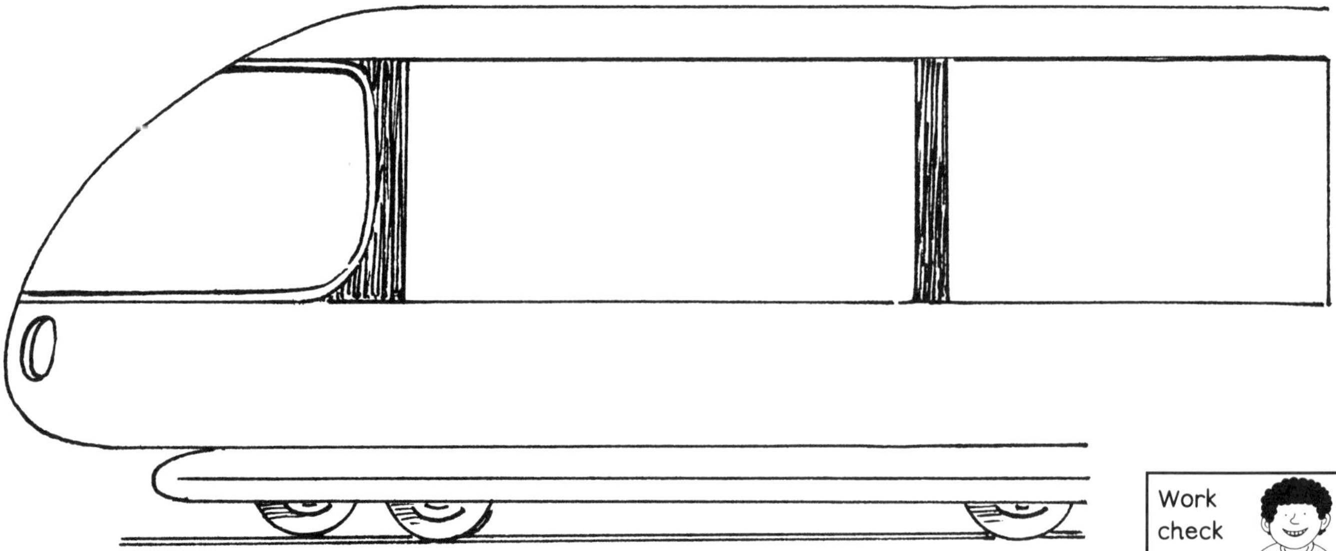

Work check

Name ______________________ Date ______________

Work check

Name ______________________ Date ____________ A T Y1/T3

Choose a story about the children at home or at school.

Draw the cover here.

Finish this sentence:

I like this story because

....

....

....

....

Choose a magic adventure.

Draw the cover here.

Finish this sentence:

I like this story because

....

....

....

....

Which book do you prefer? Finish this sentence:

The story I like best is ....

because ....

....

Work check

T8 to compare and contrast stories with a variety of settings

Name ______________________ Date ______________ A T Y1/T3

Inside, outside by Richard James
(from *More Catkins Poetry,* Playtime Poems page 14)

When I'm sitting in class
I can't wait to get out,
To run and to chase
And to scramble about.

When I'm out in the cold
And the shivers begin
And the wind and the rain –
I can't wait to get in.

There is a wet playtime in this book.
Do the children go outside?

Who has more fun at playtime,
the girl in the poem or
the children in the story?

The story and the poem are both about

....

The story is different from the poem because

....

I like the .... best

because ....

....

Work check

Name ______________________ Date ____________ Y1/T3

Read this poem.

Add to the list of more shoes and what they do.

Then write verse two. You could keep the last four lines the same.

Footsteps by Julie Holder

(From *Acorns Poetry, Sounds Poems* page 12)

Boots tramp,
Wellies stamp,
Slippers slap,
Flip-flops flap,
Trainers squeak
On shiny floors.
Bare feet pad, pad, pad,
Like paws.

....

....

....

....

....

....

....

....

Ideas for verse two

More shoes:

Football boots
Ballet shoes
Roller blades
Ice skates

What they do:

kick
point
slide
glide
dance

Work check

Long vowel sounds *ie* (page 84), *oo* (page 85) mixed (page 86), vowels with *e* (page 87)

Objective: Can the child use spelling patterns for long vowels – *ie*?

Activity: Ask the child to trace over the lines to make the words 'lie' and 'ride'. Point out that words using 'i' alone must end in 'e' in this puzzle. Some words may not need a second consonant, as in 'lie'. Ask the child to make as many words as possible, then to look at the blends at the bottom of the page. How many words can be made beginning with these sounds? When the child has finished, ask him or her to read the list of words to you. Are they all real words? Has the correct form of the vowel sound been chosen each time? Has the child an awareness of spellings that 'don't look right'? Note and date your observations on the back of the sheet.

Counting phonemes (page 88)

Objective: Can the child recognize the smallest unit of sound as a phoneme?

Activity: Remind the child that a phoneme is a single sound in a word. Use the sheet to look at and say the sounds in eleven. The rest of the numbers have been broken down into phonemes and the child only has to count them. Then ask the child to read and say the months of the year and count the phonemes. 'January' has been completed as an example. Does the child work confidently and accurately? Has s/he a clear idea of what is or is not a phoneme? Can the child explain to you the number of phonemes in a particular word by breaking down the word? Note and date your observations on the back of the sheet.

Stage 5 key words (page 89)

Objective: Can the child recognize on sight the high frequency words from Stage 5?

Activity: Ask the child to read the list of words for each story to you. Let the child have a coloured pencil and tick words read correctly. If all the words for a story are recognized confidently the child could colour the spine of that story. If the colour of the pencil is changed next time the child reads the words, s/he will know how many more words have been learned since last time. Write the date in the colour of pencil used, to help you keep a record of the child's progress.

Writing sentences (pages 90, 91)

Objective: Does the child understand the meaning of the term 'sentence'?

Activity (Page 90): Read the words inside the first witch's hat with the child. Then read the two sentences. Point out that a capital letter and a full stop have been used. Ask the child to read the words in the next hat and to write two sentences using these words. Then read each sentence with the child. Has s/he written complete sentences? If words are missing, does s/he notice? Has s/he used punctuation correctly? Note and date your observations on the back of the sheet.

Activity (Page 91): Talk about the characters in the stories. What does the child know about their age, their hair, their clothes, what they have done? Ask her/him to choose a person and write the name and draw the picture. Then ask her/him to write four sentences about the person, attempting their own spelling, but remembering capital letters and full stops. Then do as for page 90.

High frequency word lists for Years 1 and 2 (pages 92–95)

These lists have not been subdivided to provide coverage for Year 1 separate from Year 2. Instead words have been listed according to their length in blocks of 9, 10 or 11 words. This arrangement can be used as weekly spelling lists or for individual reference lists.

The high frequency word lists can be enlarged from A4 to A3. They can be used as follows: Select an appropriate list for your children. Cut that list from the sheet. As a class, copy each word in turn, with demonstration and reminders about formation of letters. Then fold the paper on the fold line. Either use the sheet to 'look, cover and write' each word, or ask the children to practise writing the words at home ready to be checked at school later.

Name and address formats (page 96)

Ask the children to copy their names and addresses and that of the school on to the sheet. They can then be taken home to practise both learning and writing them.

Name ______________________ Date ____________

How many words can you make?

b		d		
	ie			lie
d		k		
	i		e	ride
h		n		
	igh			
l		s		
	y			
r		t		

Use these blends to make some more words.

br ....

cr ....

fr ....

tr ....

Work check

Name ______________________ Date ____________

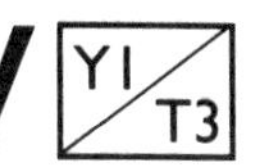

How many words can you make?

b		d		....
	oo			....
d		k		....
	u		e	duke ....
h		n		....
	ew			dew ....
m		s		....
	ue			....
s		t		....

Use these blends to make some more words with **oo**, **u-e**, **ue**, or **ew**.

bl ....

fl ....

st ....

tr ....

Work check

Name ______________________ Date ______________

How many words can you make?

cl		d
	ai	
dr		l
	ay	
gl		m
	ee	
gr		n
	ea	
h		r
	oa	
qu		s
	ow	
sm		t
	oo	
sn		th
	ew	
v		z

Work check

W1 to know the common spelling patterns for each long vowel sound

Name ______________________ Date ____________  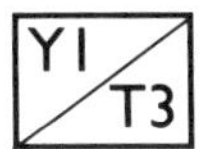

Use a-e, i-e, o-e or u-e to make words in the puzzle.

These letters are useful:
t, n, p, d, b, c, l, m

l	a	k	e						
		i							
		t			e				
		e							
							e		
				e					
									e
						e			
								e	

I made ☐ different words.

Work check

Name ______________________ Date ____________ W Y1/T3

How many phonemes?

Count the sounds you can hear in the words for the numbers.

eleven →	e-l-e-v-e-n →	6	phonemes
twelve →	t-w-e-l-ve →		
thirteen →	th-ir-t-ee-n →		
fourteen →	f-our-t-ee-n →		
fifteen →	f-i-f-t-ee-n →		
sixteen →	s-i-x-t-ee-n →		
seventeen →	s-e-v-e-n-t-ee-n →		
eighteen →	eigh-t-ee-n →		
nineteen →	n-i-ne-t-een →		
twenty →	t-w-e-n-t-y →		

Count the phonemes in the words for months of the year.

January →	7	May →		September →	
February →		June →		October →	
March →		July →		November →	
April →		August →		December →	

Work check

Name ______________________ Date ____________ W Y1 T3

Tick the words you know.

picked magic began glowing like

2 Pirate Adventure

don't help adventure Don't an

away took called about ran frightened

go out It's Go everyone my

5 Castle Adventure

of turned one Help into

threw over told lived were yelled

Work check

W2 read high frequency words specific to graded books

Name ______________________ Date ____________ W Y1/T3

Use words from each hat to make two sensible sentences like this:

1 Three witches were in the castle.

2 The witches were nasty.

witches
the were
castle in
nasty three a

1 ....

2 ....

locked
Chip opened
door a the was

1 ....

2 ....

the
a into
king frog
witch turned

1 ....

2 ....

the
party went
to a king
everyone had

Work check

 S6 reinforce knowledge of the term 'sentence'

Name ______________________ Date ____________

S Y1/T3

Choose a character from a story.
Write 4 sentences about him or her.

My character is ....

1 ....

....

....

2 ....

....

3 ....

....

4 ....

....

Work check

Name .... Date ....

an	....
as	....
be	....
by	....
do	....
if	....
or	....
so	....
us	....

9 words Words correct ☐

Name .... Date ....

bed	....
boy	....
but	....
did	....
dig	....
got	....
had	....
has	....
her	....

9 words Words correct ☐

Name .... Date ....

him	....
his	....
how	....
man	....
may	....
new	....
not	....
now	....
off	....
old	....

10 words Words correct ☐

Name .... Date ....

one	....
our	....
out	....
put	....
ran	....
saw	....
too	....
two	....
way	....
who	....

10 words Words correct ☐

Year 1/2 checklist of high frequency words arranged by word length - for assessment or spelling lists - 38 words

Name .... Date ....

back	....
ball	....
been	....
came	....
can't	....
don't	....
door	....
down	....
from	....
girl	....

10 words Words correct ☐

Name .... Date ....

good	....
half	....
have	....
help	....
here	....
home	....
jump	....
just	....
last	....
live	....

10 words Words correct ☐

Name .... Date ....

love	....
made	....
make	....
many	....
more	....
much	....
must	....
name	....
next	....
once	....

10 words Words correct ☐

Name .... Date ....

over	....
push	....
pull	....
seen	....
some	....
take	....
than	....
that	....
them	....
then	....

10 words Words correct ☐

Name .... Date ....

time	....	....
took	....	....
tree	....	....
very	....	....
want	....	....
were	....	....
what	....	....
when	....	....
will	....	....
with	....	....
your	....	....

11 words Words correct ☐

Name .... Date ....

about	....	....
again	....	....
could	....	....
first	....	....
house	....	....
laugh	....	....
lived	....	....
night	....	....
their	....	....
there	....	....
these	....	....

11 words Words correct ☐

Name .... Date ....

three	....	....
water	....	....
where	....	....
would	....	....
people	....	....
school	....	....
sister	....	....
another	....	....
because	....	....
brother	....	....

10 words Words correct ☐

Name .... Date ....

Days of the week:

Sunday	....
Monday	....
Tuesday	....
Wednesday	....
Thursday	....
Friday	....
Saturday	....

7 words Words correct ☐

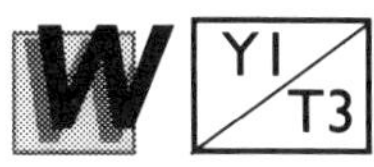

Name .... Date ....

Months of the year:

January ....
February ....
March ....
April ....
May ....
June ....
July ....
August ....
September ....
October ....
November ....
December ....

12 words Words correct ☐

Name .... Date ....

Numbers to ten:

one .... | ....
two .... | ....
three .... | ....
four .... | ....
five .... | ....
six .... | ....
seven .... | ....
eight .... | ....
nine .... | ....
ten .... | ....

10 words Words correct ☐

Name .... Date ....

Numbers to twenty:

eleven ....
twelve ....
thirteen ....
fourteen ....
fifteen ....
sixteen ....
seventeen ....
eighteen ....
nineteen ....
twenty ....

10 words Words correct ☐

Name .... Date ....

Common colour words:

red .... | ....
blue .... | ....
yellow .... | ....
green .... | ....
orange .... | ....
purple .... | ....
black .... | ....
white .... | ....
grey .... | ....
brown .... | ....
pink .... | ....
violet .... | ....

12 words Words correct ☐

Name ______________________ Date ____________ W Y1/T3

My name is ....

My address is ....

....

....

....

....

My postcode is ....

My school is ....

School address is ....

....

....

....

....

School postcode is ....